Oh, the Cases You'll Brief!

Written by D. A. Farnham, Illustrated by Emmy Grau

Copyright © 2023, Donika Alexova Farnham.

All rights reserved. No part of this publication may be reproduced, distributed, or transmitted in any form or by any means, including photocopying, recording, or other electronic or mechanical methods, without the prior written permission of the publisher, except in the case of brief quotations embodied in critical reviews and certain other noncommercial uses permitted by copyright law.

ISBN: 979-8-9858846-0-9 (Hardcover)
ISBN: 979-8-9858846-1-6 (Electronic)

Library of Congress Control Number: TXu 2-312-112

Any references to historical events, real people, or real places are used fictitiously. Names, characters, and places are products of the author's imagination.

Written by Donika Farnham
Illustrated by Emmy Grau
Front and back cover images by Emmy Grau
Book design by Donika Farnham and Emmy Grau

Printed in the US and Canada. First printing edition 2023.

LeadHer Publishing
Muskoka, Ontario, Canada.
leadherpublishing.com

Oh, the Cases You'll Brief!

Dedicated to Michael.

Thank you for your friendship, for your compassion, and for your love.

Forever and Ever.

"B" is for: Books, and Break-Ups, and Briefs.

Despite your sweet
But misguided beliefs
Each SUB-JECT you learn
Will surely demand:
You have its Case book,
    And Code book,
        And Rule book at hand!

You'll learn the way of the book.
Your social life will be took.
Your mental scape will be shook
By legal gobbledygook!

Not a friend will relate,
Not OPEN to debate:
Your-life as YOU knew it???
    -DONE for!
      Game Over!
        Checkmate!

You'll learn the way of the brief.
You'll learn that time is NO thief; you'll waste none,
But you'll find: an UNDUE share of grief.

While I.R.A.C. you perfect
And your BAE you neglect
There'll be no TIME to connect,
There'll be no THING to reflect!

How this quest will result??
No one really can say
    Whether you'll be rich,
      Or itch,
        Or a bitch some day!

One thing is clear.
One thing without question:
This dream, this pursuit becomes an obsession...

"C" is for: Caffeine, and Contracts, and Crushes.

And Covenants
That restrict ALL the light touches.

As Contracts you learn
Of languages Broiler Plate
With big cups: You'll caffeinate.
The reading: Will isolate.
Your temper: Will detonate.
You'll rage AND devastate!

Friends WILL show disgust
For this new YOU you've become.
And it MAY feel un-just.
And it WILL feel quite dumb!

SO, your classmates you'll view
As NOW similar to you...

This next part's a rush!
It will seem so un-fair!
You'll develop a crush,
You may have an affair.

You may want to come clean;
Your hands WILL need a rinse...
From the mental gymnastics
That you'll do to convince:
    It was scholastic!
    Fantastic!
    Not Plastic: your trysts.
    Elastic: your morals.
    Clenched-up: your fists.

You're much different now,
I surely suspect.
Are you ready for more,
Or do you object?

"D" is for: Damages, and Duties, and Debts.

You'll take these ALL on
Be you Blondes or Brunettes!

Compensatory,
    Pecuniary,
        Consequential,
            Excess!

But WAIT!
There's more,
I don't mean to oppress!

You'll master these.
(You'll BE at ease.)

And as you learn
    ABOUT Duties
You'll be surrounded
    BY cuties!

Do. Not.
    Give-IN
    To distractions!
    (There are NO satisfactions
    In taking-on Debts.)
        Repayment? Not Yet!
            But SOON.
                THAT'S a threat!
    And it WILL cross your mind.
    And it WILL make you sweat
    And you'll think to yourself:
    "It's all worth it… I bet…"

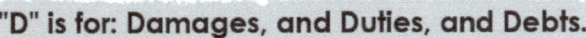

"E" is for: Extremes, and Enemies, and Easements.

And not to down-play
    All of your past achievements…
You're not perfect, you see?
LEAST of all here!
Not with THESE players.
Not with THESE peers!

There's a grade curve in place
And it's quite mandatory.
A small few will excel.
It will seem predatory.
I assure you it's not:
It is like this in life.
A few rise to the top
A few drown with great strife.

Those in-the extremes
Are seen as most lucky;
It is those in the middle
Who have it plain mucky.
You see, in the extremes
You will know where you stand;
At year's end
    You'll go on,
        Or you'll throw up your hands!

As for those in the middle?
I tell you NO riddle.
They fight about Easements:
    "In-Gross!"
    "E-quit-able!"
Competitive: the atmosphere.
    Conversations: they commandeer.
        Their interactions: insincere.
            Darwinian: This biosphere…

"G" is for: Good Faith, and Gold Dust, and Guilt.

HERE, you'll reflect on the life you have built!
Enhance?
　　　Escape?
　　　　　　Live to the hilt?

You pick up-on it, yet?
　　　　　　Life's funny lilt?

Life's funny sways?
　　　Life's bends?
　　　　　　And Life's curls?
　　　　　　　　　Life's vacillations and breathtaking swirls?

You must learn how to ride;
　　　　　How to feel.
　　　　　　　　How to steer.

And you must have deduced:
There's no permanence here.

This dance:
　　　You've seen.
　　　　　　How truths emerge from
　　　　　　　　Serotonin. Dopamine…
　　　　　　　　　　Endorphins surge with
　　　　　　　　　　　　Methylene-
　　　　　　　　　　　　　　DioxyMeth-
　　　　　　　　　　　　　　　　Amphetamine…

　　So BE safe and have fun
And take-on NO guilt!
　　　　You've worked hard and come far;
　　　　　　NO ambitions will wilt!
　　Take time for yourself,
　　And NO breach will take place
　　　　　Of YOUR solemn duty
　　　　　　To en-joy this space.

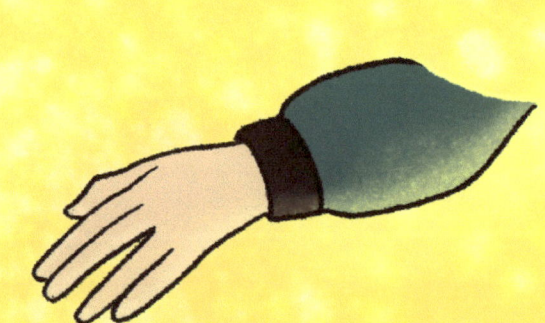

8

"H" is for: Hypos, Hypos ALL DAMN day!

And hours in study that WILL
Prove to OUTWEIGH
    The time spent
In YOUR head,
  And AT-rest,
    And AT-play!

  Slowly: Your brain matter
        Trans-FORMS to puree…

Break FREE from the madness
You WILL need a ritual:
Some THING for the vastness.
    SOME thing habitual.
      SOME thing euphoric.
        SOME thing with visuals.
SOME thing that won't leave you feeling so pitiful!
      Some run,
      Some dive,
        Some go to raves!

Explore your mind! BE so brave!
Consider the Allegory of the Cave…
Consider how Plato depicted those slaves…
Consider He who was freed; what he craved…
Would YOU have gone-back to enlighten and save???

    AND NOW?
(Surely, you see how you're like him?)
May you never stop searching for knowledge!
May you never stop seeking the light!
UPON your return from your journeys
You must SHARE what you've learned;
    (Your insights)…

"K" is for:
Karma.

(It's real so be kind...)

"L" is for: Love.

(As if you'll have time…)

"M" is for: Mantras, and Meditations, and the Make-Up

(The kind that you've hidden BE-hind)
Now, you'll WAKE-up!

From the Matrix,
  Its program,
    And the space that you TAKE-UP!!

Whose DREAMS are you dreaming?
Are they yours?? Or your mother's??

Whose LIFE are you living?
Is it yours?? Or another's??

Behind layers of make-up...
What IS it, you've covered??

Who IS the "Real You"?
(The one you trade for acceptance!)

  The one you keep hidden;
  The one who's resplendent!

    Through heartbreak, and failure,
      And loss, and transcendence:
You've learned who you are...
If NOT YET, then you're DUE!!

When was it last
YOU had a hard look at YOU??

  Do YOU like what you see?
  Can YOU make the case??

    What gifts will YOU give the world
    From this place??

"N" is for: Narcissism.

And now? And. NOW!
How long has it been??

Since YOU-last opened
 Your heart to a friend?

Since YOU-last eased
 The pain of another?

Since YOU-last helped
 A friend rediscover
  Their purpose?
   Their value?
   Their worth?
 Or let someone into YOUR earth?

The souls you meet here are quite special.
 SOME hearts you'll never forget.

In-them you'll confide and you'll nestle
And you MAY say some things you'll regret.

So be kind with your words
 Don't be reckless.

Ask questions.
Confirm what you "kNoW"!

What if all that survives is a necklace
And some flowers that died long ago??

"O" is for Opinions as well as for Outlines.

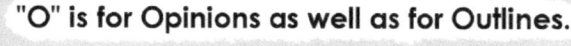

You'll read enough here for THREE-dozen lifetimes!
TWO outlines for torts!
    One-with excessive fines,
        Another for contracts,
           TWO more for crimes!

Any other kind that comes to your minds?
Perhaps...
One that defines,
    Or one that enshrines:
        YOUR thoughts of success,
        And-of gains of all kinds???

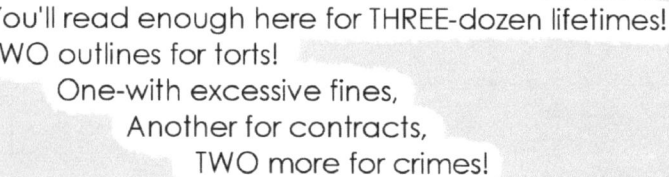

Decide for YOURSELF
What success should resemble.
It WILL NOT be easy.
It SHOULD make you tremble!
It MAY be the first time that-you disassemble:
A life plan
    That MAY NOT reflect
      What you want,
        Or what you respect!
Chase Justice!
    Chase Beauty!
        Chase truth!
           Chase whatever you want!
              BE uncouth!
              How ELSE would you dare spend your youth??

"P" is for Pain, and Purpose, and Paper.

The first is where most people's ambitions taper.
No harder to grasp than the second: is vapor!
And this is a point I hope NOT to belabor:

Under great pressure,
You KNOW what's at stake!

You'll test your own limits;
You will bend, you will break!

There will be NO time
For quiet reflection

For you KNEW this required
Nothing short of perfection...

Of course you did!! YOU?!
THESE things: you've KNOWN!!

THESE things: you've longed for
Before you were GROWN!!

Status and deference:
You've longed to be SHOWN!!

Greed? In your body:
You haven't A BONE!!

But DO NOT forget to value your work!
When hearing your rates

Some will gasp, some will smirk.
Fight for what's right!

They'll remember THIS quirk...

"Q" is for: Questions.

(As in the kind that don't quit.)
Questions: the kind that force you to submit
    To Socratic

        Methods

        And means...

Stand-UP straight, while inside you SCREAM!

    Make-YOU-feel: a MIS-FIT,
        Your professors OUTWIT
        The arguments YOU thought were clean!

    SO you'll...

QUESTION: Your IN-FER-ENCES and your claims!
QUESTION: The AUTH-OR-ITIES and the names
        Of Justices,

            Cases,

            And "Rights"...

Uncertain: you WILL spend your nights.
    But if you're brief in your notes
        And precise with your quotes
        I promise: you WILL be alright!

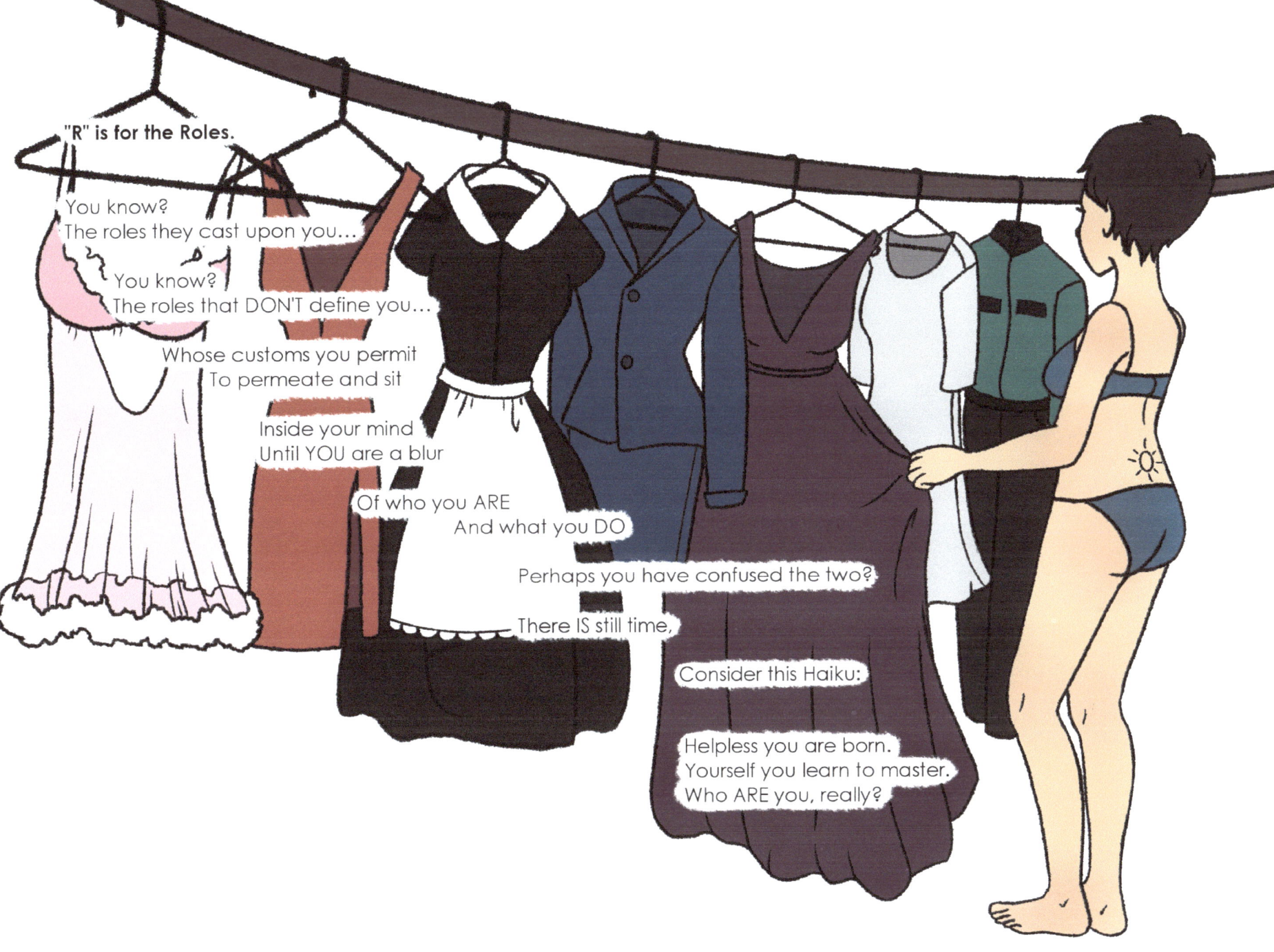

"S" is for
Sex.

(What. A. Disaster.)

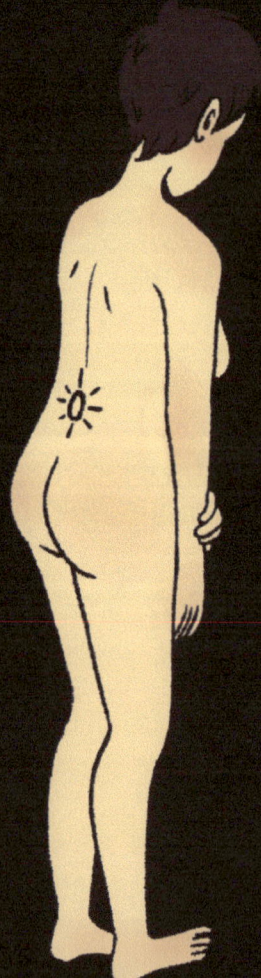

"V" is for the Void.

"What DO YOU mean?" you ask...
"What IS THIS void?" you muster...

The void is empty space...
         Immeasurable and full
            Of time,
            Of knowledge,
            Of ALL things
                It beckons and it PULLS

            It CALLS you back until it's certain
            That you've SURELY grasped

                Without a doubt, THIS IS the place
                Where minds go to UNCLASP!

                Not all things CAN be learned
                From-insides of mere books
                It is INSIDE YOURSELF
                That you must NOW learn how to look!

                INSIDE YOURSELF it's vast...
                INSIDE YOURSELF are fires!
                INSIDE YOURSELF you'll find a beast
                Who never ever tires!

                INSIDE YOURSELF it's black...
           INSIDE YOURSELF you should come BACK
        When puzzled, lost, or feeling lack!
INSIDE YOURSELF are truths!

"X" is for
X-quisite,
and
X-pensive:
This
X-istence!

Do you see your privilege?
Do you feel resistance??

Your OWN, to be exact…
You cringe at my persistence!

While others toil and grind,
A desk YOU sit behind

KNOWING that
To work is NOT to toil.

This teaching you'll have learned
In hearings long-adjourned

Before you shuffle off
This mortal coil…

"Z" is for: Zen.

My dearest of friends.
And the zeniths you'll come to
Again and again.
In three years of this ride
You'll learn MORE than just cases
MORE than just logic and rules on those pages.

Zeniths... imply NADIRS, of course.
Waves: their crests and their troughs in dual force.
Not unlike the wave,
Is law school (you've seen).
Not all of it wild.
Not all serene.
Not all experiences could be foreseen...
Life as a whole, in fact, echoes this scene!

Do you now see?
The ways of the world?
The nature of all things?
How they change? How they swirl?
How NOT to seek shelter,
But weather the storm?
And learn how to dance in the rain
And perform?

RIDE the waves; master this life!
Master composure under great strife!!
Master yourself,
Your breath and your heart.
Master the art of "stand-up and take-part!"
Master the cycles of gain and of loss,
Master this life and show her who's bos

Thank You.

D.A. Farnham

D.A. Farnham is the author of this book.

Emmy Grau

Emmy is an Oregon-based multimedia illustrator who has spent her life following her many different passions in art. She fell in love with drawing as a child and has since grown to love art in all its different forms, including printmaking, oil painting, and digital illustration.

When she isn't in her studio creating, she enjoys gardening, doing DIY projects with her husband Dan, and snuggling up with her cat friends Hazel and Atlas.

To find out more about LeadHer Publishing books and projects, or to publish a book of your own, visit
leadherpublishing.com

www.ingramcontent.com/pod-product-compliance
Lightning Source LLC
Chambersburg PA
CBHW050850010526

44119CB00016BA/358